SQUARE ROUNDS

by the same author

Plays

THE MYSTERIES
THE TRACKERS OF OXYRHYNCHUS
THE COMMON CHORUS

Poetry

THE LOINERS
PALLADAS: POEMS
FROM THE SCHOOL OF ELOQUENCE AND OTHER POEMS
CONTINUOUS
A KUMQUAT FOR JOHN KEATS
US MARTIAL
SELECTED POEMS
THE FIRE-GAP
V
A COLD COMING
THE GAZE OF THE GORGON

Theatre

DRAMATIC VERSE
THEATRE WORKS

SQUARE
ROUNDS

TONY HARRISON

faber and faber

LONDON · BOSTON

First published in Great Britain in 1992
by Faber and Faber Limited
3 Queen Square London WC1N 3AU

Photoset by Parker Typesetting Service, Leicester
Printed by England by Clays Ltd, St Ives plc

All rights whatsoever in this play are strictly reserved and application for
performance etc., should be made in writing, before rehearsals begin, to Peters,
Fraser and Dunlop, 503/4 The Chambers, Chelsea Harbour, Lots Road,
London SW10 0XF

Music by Dominic Muldowney for *The N and O Song*, *The TNT Song* and
Mourning Song on pages 63–9, reproduced by kind permission of Faber Music
Ltd. All rights in Dominic Muldowney's music for this play are strictly reserved
and application for performance etc should be made to Faber Music Limited,
3 Queen Square, London WC1N 3AU

A CIP record for this book is available from the British Library

ISBN 0–571–16868–X

2 4 6 8 10 9 7 5 3 1

For
my son
Max

Square Rounds was first performed at the Olivier Theatre, London, in October 1992, with the following company:

MUNITIONETTE/SIR WILLIAM CROOKES	Gillian Barge
MUNITIONETTE	Jo Cameron Brown
MUNITIONETTE/MUSICIAN	Helen Chadwick
MUNITIONETTE/MUSICIAN	Mary Chater
MUNITIONETTE/SIR HIRAM MAXIM	Paola Dionisotti
MUNITIONETTE/CLARA HABER	Maria Friedman
MUNITIONETTE/HUDSON MAXIM	Jenny Galloway
MUNITIONETTE	Elaine Hallam
MUNITIONETTE	Sue Holland
MUNITIONETTE/FRITZ HABER	Sara Kestelman
MUNITIONETTE	Sonya Leite
MUNITIONETTE	Maggie McCarthy
MUNITIONETTE	Myra McFadyen
MUNITIONETTE	Jane Nash
MUNITIONETTE	Theresa Petts
MUNITIONETTE	Juliet Prague
MUNITIONETTE	Emma Rogers
MUNITIONETTE	Mandy Short
MUNITIONETTE/JUSTUS VON LIEBIG	Sian Thomas
MUNITIONETTE/LADY NELLIE CROOKES	Angela Tunstall
MUNITIONETTE	Catherine White
SHELL-SHOCKED MAN & CHINESE MAGICIAN	Arturo Brachetti/ Lawrence Evans
SWEEPER MAWES	Harry Towb
MUSICIAN	Catherine Edwards
MUSICIAN	Wendy Gadian
MUSICIAN/MD	Helen Ireland
MUSICIAN	Irita Kutchmy

Director	Tony Harrison
Designer	Jocelyn Herbert
Music	Dominic Muldowney
Stage Manager and Assistant to Tony Harrison	Trish Montemuro
Choreographer	Lawrence Evans
Lighting	Mick Hughes
Magic Consultant	Ali Bongo
Costume Transformations	Arturo Brachetti
Musical Metamorphosist	Ian Dearden
Company Voice Work	Helen Chadwick
Production Manager	Annie Gossney
Staff Director	Rosalind Hickson
Deputy Stage Manager	Fiona Bardsley
Assistant Stage Managers	Valerie Fox
	Andrew Speed

This work was developed at the National Theatre Studio.

PART ONE

A circle of white surrounded by a black circle. It could be read as a 'deconstructed' top hat. Behind, the three Olivier shutters, white with black edges, like blank funeral cards.

Enter two MAGICIAN/MUSICIANS *into the Olivier 'ashtrays' and stand before their respective squares of white.*

The MAGICIAN/MUSICIANS *wear black frock-coats and top hats, very formal.*

The two MAGICIAN/MUSICIANS *flourish their wands/ drumsticks in the manner of traditional magicians but with suggestion of both percussionist and conductor.*

From the centre back shutter (black art) enter five SCIENTIST/ MAGICIAN/FUNERAL DIRECTORS *dressed in the formal outfit of frock-coat and top hat that suggests all three functions.*

They are extremely solemn, dead-pan, doleful, with the bearing first of Edwardian funeral attendants. They each wear a silk handkerchief of the purple colour associated with mourning. They each have a cane.

They pass through a 'funeral march' choreography which entails removing and replacing top hats with formal reverence, walking with the funeral march step, sudden freezes, and turns towards audience, stopping to remove their purple silk handkerchiefs to dab first their right eye then the left in a formal expression of grief. Then they replace the purple silk handkerchiefs.

In the beat after this moment of solemnity a red poppy appears in each frock-coat buttonhole.

More formal steps, funereal, as though the buttonholes had not appeared.

In succession the five canes carried by the SCIENTIST/ MAGICIAN/FUNERAL DIRECTORS *rise and become vertical. But the five remain 'funereal'.*

Five SCIENTIST/MAGICIAN/FUNERAL DIRECTORS *do various*

I

cane routines. They walk. They stop. They remove their purple silk handkerchiefs and all five are turned with a dead-pan flourish into chlorine gas silks and are put away in the breast pocket.

Exit behind black velvet square the five SCIENTIST/MAGICIAN/ FUNERAL DIRECTORS.

As they exit we hear the voices of six WOMEN *singing in German, French and English. They sing:*

> I will give my life for peace
> Ma vie je donne pour la paix
> Ich gebe mein leben für frieden

They emerge on the black velvet revolve waving German, French and English flags.

The revolve carries them behind the black velvet square and they re-emerge as NURSES *standing each beside a white square box painted with the red cross. The six boxes are distributed equally round the black revolve.*

The NURSES *pass behind the black square and instantly re-emerge as six* MUNITIONETTES. *They sing:*

> Tri–ni–tro–to–lu–ene

The six MUNITIONETTES *open the red cross boxes and take out parts of the Maxim machine gun, which they assemble rapidly and leave pointing towards the audience downstage centre. They sing:*

> The greatest life-saving machine

Re-enter the five SCIENTIST/MAGICIAN/FUNERAL DIRECTORS *with canes. They present their top hats and canes with dead-pan solemnity. Finally their canes turn into national flags, two Union Jacks, two German, and the* SCIENTIST, *who will be* HUDSON MAXIM, *points his cane at the stage with a flourish and produces an explosion and smoke.*

They all disappear. Into the smoke cloud come the Toilet Cabin and SWEEPER MAWES, *coughing and sweeping.*

SWEEPER MAWES

(*Coughing as the smoke clears*)

When you're a wheezing old geezer, you get like this,
rattling phlegm like this machine gun here, and you start
thinking the globe's got less oxygen in it to breathe than
when you weren't a wheezing old geezer. But it's not that
that life-giving gas gets in any less short supply but the
bronchials can't process it. That and a bit of irritation from
the TNT. The air's bad in here and I can't wait to get back
to my garden and dig the horse muck in for my veg and
flowers. Not that there's that much horse muck about these
days.

Thought it were just a craze, them motor cars. But no,
they seem to be here to stay. And if they do there'll come a
time when horse manure will be very hard to come by, a
precious commodity. And then there's all them horses
dropping dead at the front when their cavalry riders rush
them at the machine guns. They're finished as a fighting
force, the horse. Sir Hiram's machine here saw to that.
And no horses, no horse muck! The *Horse & Hound* lot
were a bit hard to convince at first but the Hun version of
Sir Hiram's little invention soon made them change their
ideas. There's a lot of good stuff for the garden lying out
there useless, hoof and horn, leather, blood and shit all do
a power of good to the soil. All gone to waste! Too old,
me, to have seen it for myself. I do my bit back here.
Sweep the factory floor. Full of lasses now, the factory.

You'll see women doing roles they've never done before.
The roles of the men who are out there fighting and dying.
We call the lasses canaries not because of their sweet
singing, but they do sing sweetly and it stirs my heart. We
call them our canaries because they all have a yellowish
tinge from something in the TNT. I sometimes feel I'm in
China.

Girls filling shells with TNT, assembling the parts of Sir
Hiram's gun. Women doing men's jobs. It's all very
creepy. From duchesses to plumbers' wives. Hundreds of
'em. It makes me glad to get out of the factory into my

garden, and when the odd rare horse trots by and shits, out I go with my bucket. And I get fresh air, though I don't absorb it well, with my little churchyard jobs, scything round the headstones. Very busy the churchyard and the church. A new boom really with all the lads dying out there and the womenfolk, the wives, the daughters, sisters, aunts all wanting some sort of consolation. There's a lot of praying going on. People you'd never see before the war. Congregations full of wheezing old geezers like me and the rest women and girls, and the maimed and the shell-shocked like this lad here. You can still see the war in his eyes. When he stops and stares for ages it's as if he still sees all his mates blown into pieces. The same thing with the factory. Girls. Putting Sir Hiram's machine together, putting the Maximite into the shells. I suppose they help the effort, these Dilutees, but from my point of view they're probably more bother than they're worth. First special overalls, and special cabins for taking a piss in. Toilet cabins! Toilet Cabins! And visits to the lady doctor when they get the cough. Everybody gets it. It's the powder, the TNT, the *Maximite*. I've got it but I don't go running to the doctor. And I don't wear one of them veils or respirator things. My lungs are done for anyway. So are Sir Hiram's by the sound of his hacking cough. Sounds like his invention. His gun, I mean. He's just brought out another invention. He lent me it. Let me have a puff of it when he heard me wheezing. His inhaler. His pipe of peace. Works ever so well. He's never without it. 'Have a try of my little invention, Mr Mawes,' he says, 'Your bronchia sound as wonky as my own.' Well, he talks like that. He's a . . . was an American before he settled here. Because we appreciated him and his little invention. This one. And I appreciated his inhaler too. There's this one dictates the progress of the present war, and the other helps wheezy old buggers like me, and them coughing women on the TNT. Wait till the men come back there'll be bother. Toilet cabins! And who's the poor bugger has to clean them out? You've guessed it.

Toilet cabins!

(The toilet flushes thunderously. The sound of the flush has scarcely died away when the door bursts open and there enters one of the SCIENTISTS *in the same formal dress. He is the one we will later recognize as* FRITZ HABER.*)*

FRITZ HABER
Nein! Nein! Nein!

SWEEPER MAWES
I'll ring the cops!

FRITZ HABER
Nein! NEIN!
What you've been saying may be very fine
but you must obey the rules . . .

SWEEPER MAWES
Whose rules?

FRITZ HABER
Mine!
Which means you have a rhyme on every line.
Look I'm a German and I've done four rhymes in a row.
If you can't produce the rhymes I'll have to go
and if you make Fritz Haber disappear
fertility won't be freed from the atmosphere.
So my first condition for appearing on this show's
to stamp a strict *verboten* on all prose.
These are the rhyming rules I'm known to set
for my assistants with the test-tube and pipette.
They grumble, sure enough, but I have to insist
that making verse is easy for the superior scientist.
And though I'm a modest *Mensch* I ought to mention
that I'm the reigning maestro of invention,
and, by making nitrogen materialize
out of the blue, apparently empty, skies . . .

*(*FRITZ HABER *reaches into the air and produces 'nitrogen'*

5

represented here by a light blue silk which turns slowly into dark blue and then black.)

> I'll harness its newly freed fantastic power
> to make infertile fields and wastelands flower.

(FRITZ HABER *produces from the black silk a voluminious wheatsheaf.*)

> And who benefits but you who bemoan the dearth
> of fertilizing matter to enrich the tired earth.

(FRITZ HABER *presents the wheatsheaf to* SWEEPER MAWES.)

> After the mental struggle of nitrogen fixation
> I turn to verse as an effortless relaxation.
> So, you wheezing geezer with your hacking cough
> either you get inspired or get off.

(SWEEPER MAWES *girds his loins to do his bit for his country in the poetical battle with the intruding Hun.*)

SWEEPER MAWES
(*Desperately inventing*)
> Just 'cos my bronchia get wonkier and wonkier
> don't think that I can't recite.
> For a poetical scrap you've picked the right chap . . .
> Once I've got enough wind for the fight.

> No Bosch defeats heirs of Byron and Keats
> Shakespeare makes us all Prosperos
> So square up for rounds of metrical sounds
> How about that? That's not prose!

> Every Brit can do his bit
> in ballad or monologue bouts.
> We hear verse all the time in pantomime
> and we don't need no lessons from Krauts!

6

FRITZ HABER
(*Languidly and effortlessly copying the metre*)
  Everything we do is better than you
  (as you'll find out in this War!),
  My simple request is that you do your poor best
  and versify what you said before.

  Versify the dearth of fertilizer . . .

SWEEPER MAWES
  Mark my words, we're short of turds . . .

FRITZ HABER
(*Moving towards Toilet Cabin*)
  While I do urgent business for the Kaiser.

(FRITZ HABER *goes into the Toilet Cabin and closes the door.*
SWEEPER MAWES *goes too late to try to stop him.*)

SWEEPER MAWES
  Not while I'm the toilet supervisor!

(SWEEPER MAWES *tries the door of the Toilet Cabin. Locked. He
hears farts modulating into the sounds of World War I
explosions etc. He bangs on the door. No response.*)

SWEEPER MAWES
  If they find out I've let a Kraut
  crap in their cabin I'm done . . .

(*To* FRITZ HABER *inside Toilet Cabin*)

  I don't keep that latrine spotlessly clean
  to have it befouled to some Hun.

(*Bangs on Toilet Cabin door*)

Come on out! Come on out! You trespassing Kraut
Come on out here and surrender
People like you are barred using that loo
'cos 1, you're a Gerry and 2, the wrong gender.

(HABER*'s head in red munitionette cap appears round door and
we see a sleeved arm with red cuff.*)

FRITZ HABER

No, the gender's OK, so please go away
and don't bother a girl while she's peeing
but beware when I'm done, I'll be back as the Hun.

SWEEPER MAWES

(*To audience*)
I don't quite believe what I'm seeing.

It's that sandwich (sardine!) from the factory canteen
that makes me think there's a Gerry in there.

(*To* FRITZ HABER *inside the Toilet Cabin*)

Out of that latrine or Sir Hiram's machine
'll soon get you moving, *Mein Herr*.

(*Goes to Maxim gun*)

The gun's trained on the door. I'll count ten then no more
then you'd better start saying your prayers.

FRITZ HABER

(*From within the Toilet Cabin*)
I'll come out on condition, once I've finished my mission
you'll tear up your *Times* into squares.

(SWEEPER MAWES *begins to tear* The Times *into toilet paper
squares.*

8

SWEEPER MAWES

Yes, read while you're shitting how the Krauts are committing
Atrocities in this here report.
Read this condemnation of the German nation –
But I'll hang on myself to the Sport.

(*The squares begin disappearing one by one under the door.*)

SWEEPER MAWES

You don't have to use the whole bloody news!

(*Flush from inside*)
Now will you surrender?

FRITZ HABER
NEVER!

(FRITZ HABER's *'Never!' is delivered with some force from the
centre gangway of the Olivier.* FRITZ HABER *is now in Prussian
army helmet and greatcoat.* SWEEPER MAWES *swings round
aghast. The door of the Toilet Cabin swings open and is empty of
everything but the copy of* The Times *intact and whole and
untorn into squares.*)

FRITZ HABER
(*From Olivier gangway*)
It's a smart man outwits the fabulous Fritz
the greatest/chemist inventor ever.

Now please do as I asked you. Please obey
and put some verse *spritz* into the play.
Make fertilizer the theme of your oration
unless you want an instant perforation.

SWEEPER MAWES
(*Wheezing he inhales the Pipe of Peace*)
I fertilize my garden, but my source
the earth-enriching rear-end of the horse

and what, say, a passing milk dray nag might drop
seems, as like as not, about to stop,
with cars, once faddish, pushing out the horse
which long since finished as a fighting force
is still being ridden against the fire
of guns like this one safe behind barbed wire.

All that fertilizer: hoof, leather, blood
that might have done the earth a bit of good
just left there to fester in the stinking mud.

FRITZ HABER
And for all that wastage you should lay the blame
on the Maxim who gave this dreadful gun his name,
Sir Hiram, the ex-Yankee British knight
and his brother Hudson Maxim's *Maximite*.

SWEEPER MAWES
This machine upheld our Empire, spread our civilization
It's very much indebted to Sir Hiram is our nation.
And for keeping you aggressive Huns at bay.

FRITZ HABER
I fear that that will change almost any day!

SWEEPER MAWES
And personally I owe him every breath I take
because our scientific gentleman took time to make
this inhaler to which I owe my very breath
and without it I'd cough myself to death.

FRITZ HABER
Then give yourself a rest and let's go back 50 years before
the outbreak of this present wasteful war
and consider fertility with von Liebig, chemist and
    professor
a fellow German I am proud to call my predecessor.

SWEEPER MAWES
(*Taking up broom, moving defensively forward*)
>   If he comes down here I'll cut short his career
>   this spot wasn't made for Kraut sermons
>   von or no von he's not coming on.
>   I'm guarding this space against Germans.

FRITZ HABER
(*Still from Olivier gangway*)
>   You can't keep him off, a man with a cough
>   only Sir Hiram's glass pipe keeps at bay.
>   So how will you fare when you're desperate for air
>   once I've spirited your gadget away!

(*The glass Pipe of Peace disintegrates as if by 'magic'.* SWEEPER MAWES *brandishes his broom.*)

SWEEPER MAWES
>   I'll stand with this broom like Gordon of Khartoum
>   and fight you two Krauts to the death.

(SWEEPER MAWES *wheezes.*)

FRITZ HABER
>   That won't be so easy for a geezer so wheezy
>   and so desperate to draw the least breath.

(FRITZ HABER *'turns' the broom that* SWEEPER MAWES *is brandishing into a Union Jack.*)

FRITZ HABER
(*Singing*)
>   I'm off to devise a little surprise
>   something that's certain to stun
>   all those who thought that war's only fought
>   with things like that vulgar gun.

(*The* MUNITIONETTE *who is to be 'transformed' into* JUSTUS VON
LIEBIG *gets up and enters the Toilet Cabin. The Toilet Cabin
door opens and out comes* JUSTUS VON LIEBIG *who creeps up
behind* SWEEPER MAWES, *who is frightened and runs off leaving
the Union Jack on stage.*

   JUSTUS VON LIEBIG *picks up the Union Jack as though it is a
distasteful object and pokes it with his cane down the toilet in the
Toilet Cabin. He pulls the chain. In the thunderous sound of the
flush he reads* The Times *walking round the reverberating cabin.
When he re-emerges the paper has changed from* The Times *to a
German paper with old German lettering. He pauses. He folds
up the paper. He surveys the British audience before him like
people guilty of some grave crime.*)

JUSTUS VON LIEBIG (1803–73)

>   Your nation, Britain, has left the world less green
>   by making universal the use of the latrine.
>   And who am I who tells you so?
>   One who died two hundred years ago.
>   Regrettably unrecyclable and long ago quite rotten
>   and, alas, but for a few, historically forgotten,
>   as I can ascertain when I announce my name:
>   JUSTUS VON LIEBIG PhD! Who,
>   I hear all of you enquiring in 1992?
>   Justus von Liebig PhD, FRS, analyser
>   of plant nutrition and pioneer synthesizer
>   of the much acclaimed first artificial fertilizer.
>   (And judging from those three rhymes in a row
>   pretty good at poetry in a lingo I don't know.)
>   Before I came along the process was unknown
>   for making fertilizer phosphates out of bone.
>   I extracted phosphates from skeletal remains
>   and I hasten to explain before some Britisher complains
>   in the usual prejudiced platitudes about
>   (in this case anachronistically) the Kommandant-type
>   Kraut,
>   that we Germans used bones only from abattoir and zoo
>   and rather drew the line at human residue,

a line the British nation never drew
when it dug up the bones of the dead of Waterloo
replenishing with the bones of those who'd died
all the goodness Britain flushed down into the Wash and
    Clyde.
The dead of Leipzig, Waterloo and the Crimea
ended strewn about Great Britain because of this cabin here.
Your nation, Britain, has caused the grave depletion
of its fields' fertility by waste of its excretion.
As a famous German chemist I issue the precaution
that this cabin creates havoc of Noah's Flood proportion.
Each pull of the chain is like a Noah's Flood
taking in its cataracts so much nutritious good.
What gets flushed away in these gallons of Flood water
in terms of drowned potential amounts to wholesale
    slaughter.

Your Herefords get flooded out before they get to taste
all those potential pastures your plumbing puts to waste.
In every flush the cabin makes I hear the sound
of beefy butcherable Friesians irrevocably drowned.
Whenever a Munitionette goes in and pulls the chain
it's like drowning cattle and inundating grain.
England's green and pleasant land will be laid bare,
because of the contraption inside that cabin there,
a disaster it has fallen upon us Germans to repair.
Even from 1840 I predict
that this cabin will make England agriculturally derelict.

If these *Fraulein* will assist I'll give you the gist
of atmospheric composition
how gases regulate our earthly fate
gases essential for life and nutrition.

Two gases share the domain of the air:
Oxygen essential to men
in the ratio of 22 per cent O
to 78 per cent Nitrogen N.

(JUSTUS VON LIEBIG *produces a black silk*.)

> This black silk in my left hand let's make it stand
> for the NITROGEN no man inhales
> and let this white I produce in my right
> stand for OXYGEN without which life fails.
>
> You see that the white'll prove to be vital
> to breathing to speech and to song
> and Nitrogen (N) though essential to men
> can't support life for too long.

(MUNITIONETTES *sing or breathe harshly according to whether a black or white silk is produced*.)

> It's a nutritional fact we need to extract
> our nitrogen out of the ground
> There's plenty up there all about in the air
> but down here not enough to go round.
>
> And so I am afraid we're dependent for aid
> on legumes like the pea and the bean
> and the nitrates they give to ensure that we live
> get flushed away in dung and urine.

(*Regards Toilet Cabin*)

> A constant dung torrent seems only abhorrent
> to those without chemical grounding.
> If we learned to re-use all our residues
> the yields in our fields would be astounding.
>
> One residue is still taboo
> and that's that sack of chemicals, man.
> Though a corpse once decayed could be resprayed
> through the rose of a watering can.

I look to the day maybe far away
When through the genius of Germany
all that men waste will be replaced:
a genius chemist like me!

I am the German gent who was first to invent
fertilizers with chemistry.
Phosphates lost to man down your lavatory pan
was replaced by my formulae.

GAS is so versatile both vital and vile
the air we breathe the most basic of riches
and gases extend to our other end
the base gases that billow our breeches.

The British nation has the reputation
unlike us Germans of being without
a sense of fun and if you had one . . .

MUNITIONETTES
We won't cackle at cracks from no Kraut!

(JUSTUS VON LIEBIG *produces a silk which is two parts black and
one part white from the separate black and white silks of
Nitrogen and Oxygen.*)

JUSTUS VON LIEBIG
(*Singing*)
But if two parts of N go with one of O
we get N_2O or Nitrous Oxide
and if I pass round this Laughing Gas;
you'd laugh even if your mother had died.

You'll laugh like a drain even at pain
you'd greet a dour funeral with shrieks
you'd even guffaw your way through this war
when the tears roll down everyone's cheeks.

Even one whose gaze in recent days
has looked on the worst men can know
would giggle, guffaw at the things that he saw
with one whiff of N$_2$O.

You'd see a man choke and think it a joke
you'll giggle and smirk like Mad Hatters
and Nitrous Oxide would make you deride
all solemn and serious matters.

So I'll lay aside the Nitrous Oxide
our subject's too serious for that.
We need solemnity, awe, not manic guffaw
so no one must touch that top hat.

(*Exit* MUNITIONETTES. SHELL-SHOCKED MAN *stares at top hat.*)

(*Speaking*)

Even you whose gaze in recent days
has looked on the worst men can know
would giggle, guffaw at the horrors he saw
with one whiff of N$_2$O.

You flush away your phosphates then have to despoil
the graveyards of Europe to re-enrich your soil.
You British took my phosphate extracting schemes
to what must seem quite barbarous extremes.
What we derived from knacker's yard or abbattoir
Britain raids old battles for, which is going rather far.
To make up for lost excrement your country exhumes
tons of skeletons at rest in Sicilian catacombs
to grind up fine, add acid to, and scatter
over your fields as fertilizing matter.
Your fields are so depleted it will probably take millions
of battlefield skeletons and pulverized Sicilians.
No laughing matter! A precedent of that sort
could be rather dangerous with a World War being fought!

We Germans make a little joke that in Britain RIP
means 'Rendered into Phosphates'! But confidentially
most of us are aware how well the flowers grow
when there's a compost of old corpses rotting there below
and that a corpse's soil-enriching powers
may be prodigally wasted just pushing up the flowers.
Yet even with the British who have broken through,
desperate for phosphates, that traditional taboo
I've noticed the inhibition still extends
to never making phosphates out of family or friends.
To the concerned observer what it seems you do
when desperate for phosphates you break that old taboo
is that you prefer employing as phosphate feeds
the bones of those you relegate as 'lesser breeds'
those you are able to consider not quite kin,
the Mediterranean types with slightly darker skin.
No inhibitions there to send the bone-collectors in.
Maybe in the future in another 1000 years
you taboo-breaking British may be seen as pioneers
who showed the world to triumph over superstitious awe
and dared to do what no nation dared before
and try to make good use of the human waste of war.

Speaking for myself, as a scientist, I find
little objection if my corpse could serve Mankind
but while death is hedged about with reverential awe
there's nothing we're allowed to use these empty vessels
    for.
A taboo is at the moment a taboo
and we Germans cannot break it as you British do.
The corpse of a chemist could cherish the ambition
of returning his chemicals to the cycle of nutrition
and by personal example end current superstition.

It is a fundamental truth that when we die
what's left of us could foster the dwindling food supply.
And somewhere I would like to be of use and in a modest
    way

do fertilizer duty in my process of decay.
But a taboo is at the moment a taboo
and we Germans mustn't break it as you British do.

I've had the fantasy that my phosphates might supply
phosphorescent glow enough for reading poems by.
A beacon of my bones whose radiant gleam
blazons forth the message that Science can redeem,
a symbolic torch that shows a scientific way
beyond superstitious darkness to redeem decay.
This timely but I trust not truculent tirade
comes from a body some four decades decayed
and I have to advise you as a serious scientist
that what you've been seeing can't possibly exist.

JUSTUS VON LIEBIG *exits into the Toilet Cabin. The toilet flushes
thunderously fading into the sound like a distant storm or the
distant sound of war explosions. The lights fade up. The Toilet
Cabin door opens.*

Enter SIR WILLIAM CROOKES *OM, FRS, DSC, LLD. He adds
SIR to the WC sign on the door then adds OM, FRS, DSC,
LLD. He is holding his purple handkerchief to his nose. He
'processes' downstage. He begins to introduce himself:*

Sir William Crookes OM, FRS, DSC, LLD,
Here to address the problem of the coming century.

The Toilet Cabin flushes again and two ACADEMICIAN/
SCIENTISTS *enter.*
SIR WILLIAM CROOKES *begins again and again the Toilet
flushes and four* ACADEMICIAN/SCIENTISTS *enter.*
*When the 'academy' is complete and settled the Toilet Cabin
goes down trap and the 'Black Art' box, which is like the dais
and black board of a lecture hall of a scientific academy, is
trucked on with* LADY NELLIE CROOKES. SIR WILLIAM CROOKES
walks towards his wife as the ACADEMICIAN/SCIENTISTS
applaud. LADY CROOKES *is wearing a magenta dress. Two*

18

LABORATORY ASSISTANTS put in place a chemical bench with apparatus consisting of boiler tubes in a rack.

SIR WILLIAM CROOKES

Redemptive chemistry which is our shared belief
is represented for me by this purple handkerchief.
You may ask why I always wear one. I'll tell you why
and how Sir William Perkin first derived the dye.

At the Great Exhibition William Perkin the inventor
showed crude coal tar makes marvellous magenta.
Both Lady Crookes and I were so impressed
by the Perkin process that Lady Crookes is dressed
in a mauve derived by it from disgusting tar
to remind us how redeemable even foul things are.
The noisome gasworks gave the garment trade
its most gorgeous colour with the chemist's aid.
This purple kerchief at my breast is to remind
me how the repulsive can be beautifully refined.
And from these radiant colours by extension
how Science redeems the world with its invention
Poisons that made the clouds above us blacker
and coated the flowing brook with stinking lacquer
that poisoned fish in tranquil stream and pond
converted by the chemist's magic wand
into something gorgeous and gracious that can gratify
draped on lady's form the connoisseur's keen eye.
I carry this kerchief as a sort of guiding star
to remember radiance resides in stinking tar
and wear this purple emblem at my breast
to stand for chemical invention at its best.
Like William Perkin I personally aspire
to metamorphose lower into higher.
His transforming coal-tar into brilliant dyes
has come for me of late to symbolize
chemistry at its most profound and true
creating radiance out of basest residue.

It is infinitely satisfying
to see what was black dreck serve the art of dyeing.

Those are the powers and forces that are needed
if the Western World is not to be superseded.
William Perkin's ingenious transformation
could have benefited the British nation
But unfortunately Great Britain still relies
on Germany for all synthetic dyes.
The coal tars of the Ruhr and Rhine
metamorphosed in industrial bulk into aniline.
If more of us in Britain had done work in
the processes pioneered by William Perkin
we would not now as a nation still have to rely
on Germany for all synthetic dye.

Like many a physical or chemical invention
pioneered by the British I could mention
Perkin's valuable synthetic dyes
which will always, for yours truly, symbolize
the magic of chemistry, Germans monopolize.

(*During what follows* LADY CROOKES *breathes in and produces sung notes.*)

To this conversion of noxious gases let us compare
what a human being can create out of mere air.
Just as gasworks' residues
give us some of fashion's most resplendent hues.
Simply by drawing air into our throats
and expelling CO_2 the voice produces notes.
How magical it seems simply to inhale
and then use an unseen gas to sing a scale.
A gas that in excess could otherwise kill
creatively transformed into tremolo and thrill
Like conjuror's silks out of black top hats
CO_2's converted into sharps and flats.
Into the throat that mix of gases goes

20

and Carbon Dioxide comes out as Berlioz.
What a miracle marvellous and rare
to make such soulful music out of simple air.
A chemical transaction that takes gas that we can't see
and transforms it into energy and do-re-mi.

ACADEMICIANS

We'd be obliged if all of you
would sing together CO_2.

SIR WILLIAM CROOKES

I want to hear a beautifully sung note
out of absolutely everybody's throat.
And it is to those apparently empty skies
I wish us now to turn our scientific eyes.
Having now exhausted the first part of my theme,
namely the power of chemistry to redeem
substances appalling, abhorrent, foul or base
I must now pass to a grave problem that we face
a problem that will put chemistry at its best
to its most pressing, its severest test.
As your President it is my great ambition
that the coming century, freed of superstition,
will see a new world where scientific brains
will maximize man's food supplies and minimize man's
    pains.
The twentieth century which begins next year
brings with it a crisis to do with atmosphere.
I have as President to point out the appalling fact
that the wheatfields of the West are beginning to contract,
at the very moment populations are increasing
our very source of nourishment's decreasing.
Every wheatbread-eating nation
faces the dreadful prospect of starvation.
Why, you will ask, and I will tell you why –
because nitrogen is still imprisoned in the sky.
If our science, chemistry, can't master
nitrogen and fix it I predict a vast disaster.

Unless some process can be found
no wheat will grow from our impoverished ground.
Things have come to such a perilous pass
we cannot hope to thrive unless that gas,
that invisible presence in the atmosphere,
is brought down from the sky to earth down here.
And someone inventive relieves us of despair
and brings the nitrogen we need out of the air.
If we can no longer grow wheat for our bread
we will be overtaken by races differently fed,
races far more numerous without scientific brains
but who none the less subsist on different kinds of grains.
The rice-devourers of the World could supersede
the West with wheat supplies no longer guaranteed.
It may well be our sanitary sophistication
that finally sees us a defeated nation,
and when we are, nutritionally speaking, on our knees
we could well be overrun by the Chinese,
or other billions of more boisterous breeders
biding their time as our fields fail to feed us.
Liebig told us this almost fifty years ago
And did we heed his warning. Unfortunately, No!

Any chemist worth his salt or salts who feels that he can
    rise
to the occasion and draw that gas out of the skies
is sure of Europe's gratitude, and the Nobel prize!
If I were just beginning my chemical career
I would turn my scientific mind to the atmosphere
and give it all my serious attention
and try my damnedest to discover some invention
that would ensure an inexhaustible supply
of nitrogen and therefore nitrates from the sky.
So I wear purple and Lady Nellie wears magenta
to inspire the redemptive energies of chemist and inventor.

LADY CROOKES
The most magical chemistry that man will ever know

22

is the LORD's who makes the soul from bodies base and
   low.
How much more magical to set free
the spirit from the flesh. Truest chemistry!

I promise you that once I've died
I'll contact you from the other side.
And as a scientist you'll have to swear
there exists a spirit world out there.

(*The* ACADEMICIANS *'freeze'* LADY CROOKES *like someone being
hypnotized. They drape the white cloth over her. The draped
body rises, singing. Spirit instruments play in Black Box.*)

LADY CROOKES

They'll say it's just that you can't bear
to lose a loved one and you long
to bring her spirit from the air
and hear her spirit song.

What can your chemistry achieve
more beautiful than this
If you love me you'll believe
my metamorphosis.

Science only gropes its way.
It's blindfolded by life
But everything's is clear as day
to the spirit of your wife.

(LADY CROOKES *vanishes. The cloth falls into the arms of* SIR
WILLIAM CROOKES *who goes to embrace it sadly.*)

SIR WILLIAM CROOKES

O Nellie, Nellie, you are sorely missed.
I do so want your spirit to exist.

(*The white cloth begins to form like ectoplasm and grow.*

SIR WILLIAM *removes it and finds* LADY CROOKES *in a new dress.*

FRITZ HABER *enters from Black Box. He reinstates the world of chemistry by pulling down the black board on which is inscribed the formula for the Haber process of nitrogen fixation:*
$N_2+3H_2=2NH_3$.)

FRITZ HABER

What you have witnessed does not exist
not, that is, to the conscientious scientist.
You discredit the profession. It's quite bad enough
seeing your average idiot believe that stuff
but to see a scientist, a fellow boffin
think spirits can survive beyond the coffin
discredits everything that Chemistry proclaims
and casts a dreadful slur on all our names
and undermines the hard won reputation
of scientists of every kind and nation.

Unless we demonstrate that not all our kind
are prey to spirits and stay strong in mind.
So many who'd been rational before
have turned to hocus pocus since the war
the bereaved of both British and the German nation
go to séances and such for consolation.

As the war went on and deaths increased
those who profited were spiritualist and priest.
It's quite amazing what can be believed
against all scientific proof when one is bereaved.
Even a loved one's death cannot excuse
the wholesale swallowing of otherworldly views.
Science and reason get left in the lurch
and widows and sonless mothers flock to Church.
The priests of both the present warring nations
are doing rather better now for congregations.
So many who were good scientists before
have turned to religion since the outbreak of the war.

24

But my wife, my Clara, unlike Nellie Crookes,
doesn't read such rubbish, only scientific books.
What domestic joys Sir William missed
by not choosing for a bride a fellow scientist.
How fortunate I was when Clara Immewahr
hitched her wagon to my ascending star.
One of the first women to gain a DSc
in Chemistry was the perfect wife for me.

Enter CLARA HABER *with methane pipe and unbreathable gas
detector. Enter also white-coated* LABORATORY ASSISTANTS.
*Here begins the routine of the Gas Detector Romance of
chemistry, shared vision etc.*

  FRITZ HABER *pours all the coloured dyes from the Crookes'
demonstration back into the beaker and produces the Nitrogen
black silk.*

FRITZ HABER
This apparatus of acoustic vibrators
saves lives wherever coal's mined.

CLARA HABER
As work progressed, we shared every test
with science and romance intertwined.

FRITZ HABER
A vibrating membrane warns us that Methane
is at dangerous levels below
the same high note sounds when it's Nitrogen N
but the note's lower for Oxygen O.

Let Nitrogen gas be the black silk I pass
over the pipe and you'll hear
that piercing high sound that means underground
an unbreathable atmosphere.

(*The* ASSISTANTS *produce a high note.*)

25

CLARA HABER

Let Oxygen gas be the white silk I pass
over the pipe and you'll hear
the lower note that's meant to denote
when the atmosphere is clear.

(*The* ASSISTANTS *produce a low note.*

*A dance develops with black and white producing the different notes.
It becomes a dance of shared interest in science and romance.*

CLARA *stops suddenly at the spot where once stood a Toilet Cabin.*)

FRITZ HABER

A cabin stood there with polluted air
for a purpose I don't care to mention . . .

(*To audience*)

As methane's a part of every good fart
it's detected by my brilliant invention.

CLARA HABER

In that cabin began the crisis for man
which my husband's genius solved.
His brilliant mind rather left me behind
but I was thrilled by his work, and involved.

FRITZ HABER

It was so wonderful to have a wife who knew
every complex detail of the work you do
it seems to me so sad
that it was something Sir William never had.

My wife, my Clara, urged me to persevere
with fixing nitrogen from the atmosphere.
She knew as well as Sir William, as well as I
That the salvation of Mankind lay in the sky.

No, no, I don't mean that kind of salvation
from Jesus or Jehovah but from nitrogen fixation.

But when Sir William abandoned chemistry
he left the glory of discovery to me.
the process that forever bears my name
brought me international scientific fame.
And in the end I won the Nobel prize
for bringing bread out of the empty skies.

CLARA HABER
(*Singing*)
    N_2 plus $3H_2$ gives $2NH_3$

(*Speaking*)
    Nitrogen fixation giving ammonia NH_3
    Makes fertilizers, yes, but also TNT.
    Nitrogen as nitrates could make all Europe green
    But it blasts in even blacker as tri-ni-tro-to-lu-ene.
    The nitrogen you brought from way up high
    now blows the men you saved into the sky.
    Those nitrates you produced for fertilizer
    now serve the warlike purpose of the Kaiser.

FRITZ HABER
(*Singing*)
    I pioneered fixation to fulfil
    a desperate human need and not to kill
    when I pioneered the process I had in mind
    only benefits and blessings for mankind.

CLARA HABER
The golden wheat that grows out of the ground's
fed by the same nitrates as those in machine gun rounds.

FRITZ HABER
It was never, ever my intention;
to engineer more deaths by my invention.

CH: Your process led to death and devastation
FH: It saved the world that hurtled to starvation.
CH: It boosts the firepower of the nation
FH: Is that so bad? It's your country too.
CH: It's hard to feel it's yours when you're a Jew.
FH: To give new life to fields that were depleted
CH: To save the Kaiser when he almost was defeated.
FH: How could I foresee the uses to which my work was put?
    How could I, Clara, how?
CH: You couldn't see the future, you couldn't but
    it was obvious to your Frau.
FH: More fields full of wheat, more sacks of flour
    more bread, more bread.
CH: More shells, more ammunition, more fire-power
    more dead, more dead.
FH: They'll thank Fritz Haber when the crops yield
    twice as much good grain.
CH: And curse Fritz Haber on the battlefield
    with shrapnel in the brain.
FH: Without me and my invention, my dear Clara
    Europe would end up bare like the Sahara.
CH: It's a Sahara now. Its barrenness is moral.
FH: O Clara, Clara, love me, please don't quarrel.

FRITZ HABER

(*Speaking*)

    I'm only the inventor how can I guarantee
    no one will turn my nitrates into TNT?
    Duality reigns. It wasn't my decision
    to have my ammonia turned into ammunition.
    Clara, I had the noble dream of making Europe green
    with the nitrates from the process of my ammonia machine.
    I never intended it for TRINITROTOLUENE
    NH_4NO_3 and $(NH_4)_2SO_4$
    fertilizers, Clara, not materials of war.

CLARA HABER

I'm perfectly aware what those chemicals are for!

28

You're a chemist you could have easily foreseen
more and more TRI–NI–TRO–TO–LU–ENE.

(*The* MUNITIONETTES *enter on the rim revolve, filling shells.*

They are singing the syllabified TRI–NI–TRO–TO–LU–
ENE. MUNITIONETTES *close in on* FRITZ *and* CLARA *who*
disappear. There is an explosion and the MUNITIONETTE
standing behind the cloud turns into HUDSON MAXIM.)

HUDSON MAXIM

It's high time the expert appeared on the scene
if the talk's of TRINITROTOLUENE.
If you're looking for a maestro of TNT
look no further, folks, that's HUDSON MAXIM, me!

What he's gone and done that ingenious Hun
Europe's first ammonia synthesizer
is to create a supply of nitrate
for the bullets and shells of the Kaiser.

The German supplies are on the rise
when they almost had dwindled to zero
when the Brit naval forces blocked Chilean sources
so his magic made Haber a hero.

Because his side got a boost from the nitrates produced
from the endless supplies in the air
it's the year that I say to the USA
wake up, get armed and PREPARE!

MUNITIONETTES

(*Singing*)
We must prepare with TRINITROTOLUENE!

HUDSON MAXIM

Great nations thrive and arts survive
said John Ruskin in times of war

and ancient Greece was drained by peace
but buoyed up by conflicts before.

Music's best made when the barricade
is kept in a good state of repair
the arts and the senses need good defences
the message for all is PREPARE!

MUNITIONETTES
We must prepare with TRINITROTOLUENE!

HUDSON MAXIM
I was first to propose that history shows
how the laurels on Peace are kept green.
Gold, frankincense, myrrh aren't gifts for her
but TRI–NI–TRO–TO–LU–ENE.

(*The* MUNITIONETTES *sing the Trinitrotoluene Round.*)

HUDSON MAXIM
I would wish her a well-trained militia
this goddess Peace everyone loves
we're more likely to walk at peace with the hawk
than with the soft cooing of doves.

(*The* MUNITIONETTES *cough rhythmically.*)
My brilliant campaign's put into their brains
how foully their family would fare
if a foreigner lands with his lascivious hands
Now the word nationwide is PREPARE!

MUNITIONETTES
We must prepare with TRI–NI–TRO–TO–LU–ENE!

HUDSON MAXIM
And the now that I mean is 1915
Britain needs the US to save her
If the USA enters the fray
it'll tip the scales in her favour.

Brother Hiram's machine is the defence that I mean
It's the greatest life-saver that gun
because it can save many men from the grave
by getting the war quickly won.

(*The* MUNITIONETTES *begin coughing from the effects of TNT.
The* MUNITIONETTE *with the worst, most protracted fit of
coughing becomes* SIR HIRAM MAXIM.)

HUDSON MAXIM
I bet that that cough it could make him a profit
if he harnessed its force to a gun.
The hacking that racks him sounds like his Maxim
and he should point his old tubes at the Hun.

(*Enter* SIR HIRAM MAXIM *with Pipe of Peace, coughing.*)

Because, unlike mine, his health's in decline
brother Hiram turns all his attention
attempting to ease his terrible wheeze
and hence (if it's worthy the name) THAT invention.

(SIR HIRAM MAXIM *inhales his Pipe of Peace and gradually is
able to speak.*)

SIR HIRAM MAXIM
I'm ready to share it with those short of air
like our little Munitionettes in a ring.
It's so good one puff is always enough
Just suck it once and you'll sing.

(HIRAM *gives the Pipe to the* MUNITIONETTES *who take a puff
and pass it on. After one puff they sing the Trinitrotoluene
Round.*)

HUDSON MAXIM
It upsets him that Munitionettes

suffer like he does from his chest
two lady MDs tried to blame the disease
on my gunpowder which is the best.

To hell with the *Lancet*, these gels will chance it
even if their work here will mean
a few days off with a bit of a cough
caused (or NOT) by

(*Joining the* MUNITIONETTES *singing*)
  TRI–NI–TRO–TO–LU–ENE.

HUDSON MAXIM

But some of their sisters are war-resisters
and meet at the Hague as we speak
and all of them swore to stop the war
and such women make their nations weak!

There are sensitive souls who seek caring roles
the Florence Nightingales
and then there are these, your 'Dilutees'
who work in munitions like males.

SIR HIRAM MAXIM

(*After a great deal of inhaling*)
  My worst nightmare's being short of air
  and gasping for breath as you've seen
  so you'll understand if I turn my hand
  to perfecting this inhaling machine.

  If, perish the thought, future wars won't be fought
  with my weapon I'd find that depressing
  but that's not my belief so I seek relief
  for a problem that for me's far more pressing.

  My killing machine in 1915
  will stay as it is for ever
  in a 100 years no engineer's
  going to turn out a weapon so clever.

32

And my powder, his gun will get this war won
I'd like you to know who to thank.
For his help in your fight he got made a Knight
but I'm staying an undubbable Yank.

Now you're aware I'll make the US prepare
and get ready to intervene
please give your applause to that winner of wars
Sir Hiram Maxim and life-saving machine.

Only by preparation can occupation
and such like ills be prevented.
For defensive use let me introduce
the greatest life-saving instrument ever invented!

(MUNITIONETTES *sing:*)

The greatest life-saving machine

HUDSON MAXIM
Though the USA has led the way
as machine-gun pioneers
my brother knows his invention owes
a lot to a Limey dead 200 years . . .

SIR HIRAM MAXIM
James Puckle first solved how a chamber revolved
and achieved a sustained rate of fire.
In 1718 he made a machine
that killed two ways lower and higher.

HUDSON MAXIM
In his own way and in his own day
he faced the problem we face at present

SIR HIRAM MAXIM
how to use the same gun on everyone

33

HUDSON MAXIM

but distinguish the Cross

SIR HIRAM MAXIM

from the Crescent.

MUNITIONETTES

(*Singing*)

With his Protestant zeal he fashioned the steel
that got shot from his gun in two forms.
Paradox though it sounds he fashioned *square rounds*
to kill those who scorned Christian norms.

HUDSON MAXIM

If it's the Cross you revere you get killed by a sphere
but if you face towards Mecca at prayer
the pain that you'll feel pierced by James Puckle's steel
is redoubled when bullets

MUNITIONETTES

are square.

SIR HIRAM MAXIM

'For defending the Laws and the Protestant Cause'
he wrote of his gun with poetical flair
So a Catholic could fall by a spherical ball
but the ball for a Moslem was

(*Audience*)

square.

HUDSON MAXIM

In his day he'd decide how people died
according to religion or skin.
Those outside the bounds would get the square rounds
and the round rounds would slay those within.

MUNITIONETTES

He couldn't forget the Islamic threat
and got his dual weapon to work
so that normal spheres killed Christian peers
but more painful rounds killed the Turk.

HUDSON MAXIM

In this day of ours with greater powers
the question of 'square rounds' is vaster
but whatever you say of death Maxim's way
there can't be many much faster.

SIR HIRAM MAXIM
(*After using his inhaler*)

A slower death gasping for breath
my bad lungs make that my nightmare.
When I have to go I pray it's not slow
and that I don't have a harsh struggle for air.

The very worst fate I could contemplate
after years of desperate inhaling
is a scenario where I choke slow
with the atmosphere's oxygen failing.

It seems just as unfair as a round that's square
to interfere with the passage of breath.
I'd be gunned down rather than drown
or die any way than by choking to death.

HUDSON MAXIM

It's time for white knuckles when guns like James Puckle's
get into hands that are dark-skinned not fair
and then it's the white man's the one in the sight
and the round with his name on is square!

But perish the thought suppose that their sort
get a hold of my weapon and train

its muzzle toward not a primitive horde
but a platoon of pure Saxon strain.

SIR HIRAM MAXIM
(*After using his Pipe of Peace*)
When you see assegais on the distant horizon
and the Dervishes shaking their spears
you'll thank the Lord that you'll master that horde
with the inventions of Yank engineers.

HUDSON MAXIM
The gun seemed to need a 'lesser breed'
to prove its true metal or worth
and the Maxim floored the Fuzzy horde
and thousands were soon eating earth –

Let's celebrate!

MUNITIONETTES
Omdurman '98!
They say it all the figures
48 white men were killed in the fight
and 11000 niggers!

SIR HIRAM MAXIM
This gave support to the British thought
God had made them above all others
but they never could slay so many a day
without this device of my brother's.

HUDSON MAXIM
It's all very fine when the firing line
is full of blacks from the back of beyond
but men show some qualms when they use the same arms
on someone who's blue-eyed and blond!

MUNITIONETTES
The empire resounds with Maxim sounds

and the gun quells unrest and riot
the volley of shots at the Hottentots
soon gets a quotient of quiet.

Our Queen was right to make you a Knight
for the service your weapon had done
but the accolade should have been made
much better still to the gun!

SIR HIRAM MAXIM

His Grandmother, your Queen, praises my machine
to the Kaiser, a bellicose sort.
His Gran's testimonials on killing colonials
soon convinced Kaiser Wilhelm who bought.

HUDSON MAXIM

The scores and scores killed in Imperial wars
and the Knighthood bestowed on my brother
gave the gun the cachet it still has today
and the Kaiser would hear of no other.

SIR HIRAM MAXIM

So British and Hun stockpiled the gun

HUDSON MAXIM

the arsenals grew fuller

SIR HIRAM MAXIM

and fuller

HUDSON MAXIM

and round rounds

SIR HIRAM MAXIM

were squared

HUDSON MAXIM

as two white sides prepared

to kill cousins of similar colour.

MUNITIONETTES

The better the gun the sooner war's won
and guns don't come much better than ours
but the present war's a balanced see-saw
when the gun's possessed by both powers.

(*Re-enter* FRITZ HABER.)

FRITZ HABER

(*Speaking*)

I think that I may modestly say
this invention will be superseded.
In this very year I have an idea
that delivers exactly what's needed.

(*Singing*)

Here the *Mensch* is who'll get war out of trenches
and back into open terrain.
We'll force our way right through to Calais
with Haber's superior brain.

I think I'll devise a little surprise
something that's certain to stun
all those who thought that war's only fought
with things like their vulgar gun.

HUDSON MAXIM

Face up to the fact my brother's cracked
the matter of weapons for ever.
You can't outsmart the state of the art
even you who thinks he's so clever.

FRITZ HABER

(*Speaking*)

You think that you've got the best of the lot

38

I say to you modestly NEIN
because I prepare to release from the air
a little invention of mine.

(*Singing*)

The war I detest in which all the best
and bravest of men meet their fate
I do what I can not for Deutschland, but MAN
and save him before it's too late . . .

Something that shocks, unorthodox
a weapon not thought of before
a sudden surprise out of the skies
to bring a quick end to this war.

HUDSON MAXIM
I very much doubt that this curious Kraut
will be the one to surpass

SIR HIRAM MAXIM
the great inspiration of my life-saving creation
what will you do it with?

FRITZ HABER
GAS!

(FRITZ HABER *now produces from his top hat an endless ribbon of chlorine gas silk which pours over the Maxim gun downstage centre and envelops it. Gas Alarm Music.*
   The SHELL-SHOCKED MAN *picks up the top hat of Nitrous Oxide. He laughs. He turns into a WWI soldier. He laughs. He tries to stop laughing. He turns from WWI soldier into a mourning woman in black dress and black veil.*)

END OF PART ONE

PART TWO

The sound of laughter from the auditorium speakers increases.
The sound of the laughter draws from the centre back Olivier
shutter the entire company as WOMEN IN MOURNING VEILS
carrying lighted candles. MOURNING WOMEN *sing:*

> Who will bring the colour back to life
> for mourning mother and the widowed wife?
>
> When the flag-saluting nations fight
> the world is drained to black and white
>
> Black and white, black and white
> can you go on seeing the world in black and white?

On the hiss that concludes the song the candles change into silks
the colour of chlorine gas. One of the WOMEN *lifts her veil and*
reveals herself as FRITZ HABER *who collects the silks from the*
WOMEN.

FRITZ HABER
I see it now as my inventor's brief
to spare all Europe's mothers more appalling grief.
I've found a way to staunch the loss of Europe's sons
to yes, alas, my nitrates and the Maxim guns.
I've found, as some sort of penance to my wife,
a way to end the war and stop the loss of life.
I'll prove Chemistry is humanity's best friend
and by using its potential bring war to an end,
that both contestants were equally supplied
with Maxims and explosives led me to decide
to use to our advantage the chemistry that supplies
the world, from Germany, with all its brilliant dyes.
The flags and banners of Europe's warring sides
were coloured by synthetic dyes that Germany provides.

40

Germany coloured the clothing worn by all the wives
who've waved their husbands off to throw away their lives,
all the cheerful colours put away
in mothballs till what they hope is Victory Day.
Out of the industry which gives the world its dyes
I can chemically concoct a new shock from the skies.

And when I speak of dyestuffs I should know.
My father, Siegfried, dealt in indigo
and though I advised him my father couldn't see
that plants would be supplanted by my chemistry.
He couldn't foresee that colours of all sorts
could be fabricated easily in test-tubes and retorts.
He believed in Nature. His son, the doctor, knew
that indigo was finished as the world's one source of blue.
It was then I learned the processes that now can be employed
to prevent a devastated Europe being totally destroyed . . .
Clara has her scruples, moral reservation
on the use of science in the conflict between nations.
My official life is pressured my family life is nil
since Clara knew my nitrates could be used to kill.
The Prussian monarch's pressure, Clara's pique
at what she thought perversions of laboratory technique.
I apply my mind to problems and I find
that most problems can be solved by a scientific mind.

Some ingenious method had to be found
to get the entrenched troops out of the ground.
Once we're victorious and war's brought to halt
Clara might forgive what she thinks my fault
when she sees my nitrates that scorched Nature for the Kaiser
returned to crop-filled fields as fertilizer.

(*Enter* CLARA HABER.)

CLARA HABER

I gave up chemistry to serve you as a wife
now you betray our science to poison life.

The beneficial chemistry that was our bond before
broken when I saw science made to serve the war.
You, a scientist, a chemist and yet you comply
with the Kaiser's orders so that millions will die.
You, who saved Mankind from Crookes' predicted doom
may send as many as you saved into an early tomb.
Now the Kaiser commands a chemist to devise
a form of killing from those brilliant dyes
that gave my dress its sheen and elegance
that caught your eye when you asked me to dance.

FRITZ HABER

But explosives are chemical weapons too.
Mine seems terrible only because it's new!
My gas will break the deadlock, make the war much
   shorter
and therefore save millions from the slaughter.

The explosives with which the war is being fought
are simply gas weapons of a different sort.
How many times in school did you hear your class recite
when carbon, sulphur and saltpetre mixed ignite
the volume of gas, Clara, GAS increases
800 times its bulk and blows to pieces
the canister confining it, and those bits fly
and pierce men's hearts and brains and make them die.
So what has brought the war to its present pass
is simply another way than mine of using gas.
Sentimentalists assume it's all very well
if Maxim uses gases as the power to propel
a bullet through the air, hit its mark, and shatter
a man's ribcage, but quite a different matter
if I use a gaseous resource but I dispense
with the metal missile. What's the difference?
Don't they both result in death? That's the intention
of both Sir Hiram Maxim's and my own invention.
If Maxim hadn't used gas from each round fired to feed
the next round into the chamber, now there'd be no need

to use my chemical genius in order to surpass
his use of gaseous energy with my simpler use of gas.
Without gas the Maxim gun could not exist
and no need for me to counter his mechanics with my mist.
The force of explosive gas that travels very very fast
blows head and limbs off in its fearsome blast.
It's a chemical weapon, chemicals and gas
and yet the scruples of the moralist let that pass.
Make delicate distinctions but, alas,
the essential element of both is gas, gas, gas.
One gas blows to pieces, one manages to choke
its unsuspecting victims with a greenish yellow smoke.
If I were a victim's mother. Imagine being her
I know which of the two fates for my son I'd prefer.
If one were forced to make that gruesome choice
and my son were a victim then gas would get my voice.
An appalling decision but gas would get my vote
because apart from internal damage to lungs and throat
my boy would be intact, whole and I
would have a corpse for burial I could identify.
It would still be my boy, mein liebling, him
not half a helmet and one mangled limb.
It's bad enough to die but once you've died
isn't it better if your corpse can be identified?
Rather than be bits and pieces jumbled up with others
sent home to the wrong grief-stricken mothers?
The burial parties won't take time to pick and choose,
what each piece of raw meat once was or even whose.
Better in your box intact whatever your belief
if only that your mother has the right bits for her grief.
RETURNED IN PIECES is the RIP
of those who met their fates through TNT.

The metal weapons solider than chlorine's
the one that blows a man up into smithereens.
The solid weapons shatter men to little shreds
they separate their bodies and their heads.
All those solid metals propelled by force

43

are infinitely more merciful, of course! Of course!
Unlike explosive nitrates my invention won't delay
the end of hostilities day after bloody day.
The war that's now in stalemate will be at once curtailed
as soon as my invention is released and first inhaled.
In the future, if you don't, the world will come to see
that I saved millions and will one day honour me.

CLARA HABER

Honours aren't readily bestowed on Jews.
You're well aware of the Kaiser's anti-Jewish views.

FRITZ HABER

That's precisely why, Clara, that I can't refuse!

CLARA HABER

He would never have used you if he could find
a Gentile genius with your inventive mind.
He's known to call Jews vermin and parasites
and thinks of them as Africans and not as fellow whites!
Don't you realize the Kaiser will restrain
his anti-Semitic prejudice while he can use your brain.
If he could find an Aryan as brilliant as you
do you think he'd even bother with a 'bloody Jew'?
You are supping with the devil and very soon
you'd wish you'd gone to supper with a longer spoon.
He or some saner campaign adviser sees
that they can't win the war without your expertise.
Once they've extracted from you all that they can use
he'll dismiss you and detest you like all the other Jews.
Once the war is won he won't bother to conceal
he feels about the Jews as almost all the Prussians feel,
and if his Imperial Majesty permits
himself such prejudice, what hope have we, Fritz?

FRITZ HABER

I'll convert that supercilious Prussian sneering
into surprised gratitude with a little engineering.

44

Even the Junkers will finally acknowledge
the superior power of scientific knowledge.
And they sneer at civilians and despise us too
especially if like me the civilian's a Jew.
He needs my expertise, and so he reins
in his prejudice so he can pick my brains.
And the Kaiser sends the Junkers to form an anxious
    queue
to give chemical commissions to the genius Jew
who made the invisible air serve the cause of world
    nutrition
and so seems less a chemist and more of a magician.
And who will stop the war unless I go
to serve the Prussians as their Prospero?

(*Music*)

CLARA HABER

Colours in which young people's hearts rejoice
when promenading or on the ballroom floor
are the same hues that rival nations hoist
for youth to follow blindly into war.

Colours chemistry invented cheered the soul
and filled the youthful heart with rare delight
but cut up into squares up on a pole
lead the same youth to perish in the fight.

VEILED CHORUS

Can you go on seeing the world in black and white?

CLARA HABER

(*Speaking over* VEILED CHORUS)

I predict that every brilliant colour will come back
merged to one immeasurable length of widow's black.
Those piffling pennants that made us feel so proud
will be bleached by bitter tears to one long shroud.

45

(*Singing*)

> The bright flags waved by cheering crowds
> when they paraded as recruits
> are bleached now for the veterans' shrouds
> or black for veils and funeral suits.

VEILED CHORUS
(*Singing*)

> The flags now waving in the streets
> are widows' veils and winding sheets.

CLARA HABER
(*Singing*)

> Bright brilliant banners flew
> when the young men all left home
> when they return the only hue
> is a mournful monochrome.

VEILED CHORUS
(*Singing*)

> Can you go on seeing the world in black and white?

CLARA HABER
(*Singing over* VEILED CHORUS)

> It's black and white not brilliant shades
> produced now by the fashion trades.
> Black for all the waiting crowds
> who've come to claim their men wrapped in white shrouds

> Bits of cloth dipped in bright dyes
> lead Europe's youth to war.
> Cloths of black veil widows' eyes
> and shroud-length figures scar.

VEILED CHORUS
(*Singing*)

> Black and white, black and white

46

white and black, white and black,
Bright flags send them out to fight
white shrouds wrap them when sent back

CLARA HABER

(*Singing over* VEILED CHORUS)
    I predict that every brilliant colour will come back
    merged to one immeasurable length of widow's black.
    Those piffling pennants that made us feel so proud
    will be bleached by bitter tears to one long shroud.

(VEILED CHORUS *continue humming*)

CLARA HABER

(*Speaking over* VEILED CHORUS)
    The shades you adore to see us women wear
    are converted into cankers that corrupt the living air,
    the green of undergarments, the green of a chemise
    born as deadly poison on the April breeze.
    Into the top hat vats the coloured silks went in
    and out came something most unfeminine.

    Black tar from the gasworks gave the garment trade
    glorious colours with the chemist's subtle aid.
    Now the courtesan's costume, the gentleman's cravat
    come out caustic from the Kaiser's chemist's vat.
    Those materials that lovers' hands would stroke
    wafted as miasma and making young men choke.
    A scary scarf, a shawl that's death to wear
    an enveloping miasma choking off the air.
    The sheen of those Chinese silk shantungs
    choking boys and shattering men's lungs.
    A rustling undergarment, a silken Chinese shawl
    hovering above the earth as a poisonous pall.

FRITZ HABER

If not you then the world will one day see
how my invention stopped the war and will come to honour
   me.

47

CLARA HABER

If you use our chemistry as a means of killing men

(*Singing*)

you'll never see your Clara alive again.

(*The* VEILED CHORUS *echoing* CLARA HABER *sing: 'Alive Again'.* CLARA HABER *takes out the revolver.* FRITZ HABER *moves to the downstage war front and is followed at a distance by two* VEILED WOMEN. *Six Top Hats appear on the revolve and stop centre stage.* FRITZ *fills them with chlorine gas silk. These are to become the gas cylinders of the first European gas cloud in warfare.* FRITZ HABER *begins the countdown to the release of the gas.*)

FRITZ HABER

Zehn, neun, acht, sieben, sechs, funf, vier, drei, zwei,
    ein . . .

(*Two* VEILED WOMEN *pick up the edges of the green chlorine silk and trail it slowly upstage to where* CLARA HABER *is standing with the gun. The two* VEILED WOMEN *lay the green chlorine silk at the feet of* CLARA HABER *then they stoop and pick up the opposite hem and draw it upwards revealing it as a German flag which slowly covers* CLARA HABER *poised with her gun. We see the gun poised until the moment the shot is fired.*

On FRITZ HABER'*s 'ein' we hear a high 'Nein' from* CLARA *and* THE VEILED CHORUS. *This 'Nein' continues under the following speech of* FRITZ *like a death knell, or a gas alarm bell.*

From the six cylinders green smoke rises and a green silk falls to the stage behind the cylinders.)

FRITZ HABER

With my elegant invention I put to sleep
the unsuspecting enemy entrenched at Ypres.
As my silky releases hissed and swirled
for the first time ever in the history of the world

I have to confess that I felt rather proud
of the simple device of my suffocating cloud.
The Prospero of poisons, the Faustus of the front
bringing mental magic to modern armament.
Lacework lassoos on the springtime April breeze
wafted through the Maxim-shattered trees
that this spring won't see bud or put out leaves
and curled round the trunks like handkerchiefs.
And then the doldrums of trench warfare broke
when I cast over it my magic chlorine cloak.
I was elated, no, I was ecstatic
when suddenly the war stopped being static.
The stalemate that had seemed so everlasting
I broke through instantaneously by casting
my green cloud, my magic silken pall
over the panicking troops and killed them all.
So non-violent the way the green veil floats
through the atmosphere straight into men's throats.
All that Maxim weaponry so brash, so crude, so loud
was brought to a standstill by a quiet hissing cloud.
A hiss like a nest of knotted snakes,
a waft of silken veils, the frontline breaks.
My escaping cloud like a scarf out of a hat
a chorus line of canisters, and that *could* have been that.
The British line was broken we could have forced a way
straight through the enemy and as far as Calais.
Yesterday we could have had the British beat
never had a gap been so complete.

But the military *Dummkopfs* threw away
the opportunity I gave them only yesterday.
They lost the advantage and things soon went back
to the way they were before the gas attack.
I thought as I watched my cloud of doom descend
that my genius would bring the war to a quick end
and by hastening the outcome I would save
half of Europe from an early grave.
I made the opening. They threw away

a chance that might have got them to Calais.
I made the opening. But to complete the task
the German army needed a good protective mask.
The expert in this field, the one who knew
being a physiologist, exactly what to do
was, as it happens, like myself a Jew
and the military prejudice wouldn't let them use
more than absolutely necessary any Jews.
I was 'absolutely necessary' but the task
was aborted without my colleague's mask.
So because of prejudice in High Command
the army didn't gain the upper hand
but having depended on the genius of one Jew
they didn't want to feel obliged to two.
By the time the gas had cleared the chance was missed.
The enemy recovered and was ready to resist.
Now to retain the needed factor of surprise
ingenuity is forced now to devise
novel venoms to let into the skies.

(*He pauses to register the enormity of the prospect of gas escalation. Now he has to return and face* CLARA.)

I am the father of the new era that's begun
since I've shown the world the way beyond the Maxim gun.

(*The* VEILED CHORUS *begins to hum as before*.)

Oh Clara, Clara, *liebchen*, what has your husband done?
What have I fathered on the human race?
Now even more deeply dyed in my disgrace
it is my dear one I most dread to face.

(*We hear a shot from Clara's revolver. We hear the voice of the dead* CLARA *singing from behind the flag*.)

(*Recorded voice*)

Remember the whistle you invented that pulsates
in the presence of poisonous gases underground?

I am a human whistle and your dead wife's fate's
to be your new invention's warning sound.

(*The* VEILED CHORUS *begins to sing the high and low notes of the
Methane Pipe Song.*

FRITZ HABER *goes back home drawn by the voice of* CLARA
and pulls the flag away. There is no CLARA *there but the voice
continues singing from the back of the centre aisle in the Olivier
stalls.*)

CLARA HABER

(*Singing*)

The whistle, my voice, the high Cs and Ds
just within the bounds of being shrieks
will enter men's hearts now, and it soon frees
the tears to run down even manly cheeks.

I'll be your invention that redeems
the good scientist you were when we first met.
I'll be the Siren haunting men in dreams
and make their whiskered cheeks feel hot and wet.

The same brain brought both benefit and bale,
It fixed the nitrogen that fed the fields that fed
these same open mouths that now inhale
another Haber brainchild and drop dead.

FRITZ HABER

I have to tell you as a scientist
though I am wrong that you do not exist.

Though I love you you are nothing but a wraith
In which no scientist of note shows any faith.

51

(*Exit* CLARA *and the* VEILED CHORUS, *singing and repeating and fading to nothing:*)

> CLARA HABER AND VEILED CHORUS
> He'll never live to see his fellow Germans use
> his form of killing on his fellow Jews.

(*As if pulled by the voice,* FRITZ HABER *exits backwards into the future.*

Enter HUDSON MAXIM *and* SIR HIRAM MAXIM. SIR HIRAM MAXIM *has his inhaler in one hand and in the other what seems to be a broom handle with a rubber triangle flap on the end.*)

> SIR HIRAM MAXIM
> Haber broke the blockade but also betrayed
> the beliefs that Science should share.
> I'm shocked to the core that even in war
> a chemist should poison the air.

(*He wheezes. He inhales.*)

> I cannot bear that he poisoned the air
> with clouds that choked soldiers to death.
> I can empathize with a man who dies
> after a panicky struggle for breath.

(*He inhales.*)

> To interfere with the atmosphere
> can anything be more beastly than that?
> Nitrogen fixation and asphyxiation
> born out of the same top hat!
>
> Nitrates we saw for peace and for war.
> Black's always there with the white.
> One good, one bad force, from the very same source,
> the darkness contained in the light.

(*Wheeze. Long inhaling.*)

HUDSON MAXIM

(*Singing*)

He thought it obscene to kill with chlorine
it took science into realms far beyond
what a Knight with a topper thought decent and proper
so how did Sir Hiram respond?

Apart from the fits of coughing when Fritz
and his gas get even a mention
for a month after Ypres his brain couldn't sleep
till he'd come up with a counter-invention.

Never really completed it showed him defeated
a disappointed and bitter old man.
His only idea for anti-gas gear
was a broom handle attached to a fan.

Our famed engineer won't last a year
but he's filing patents in the pretence
his broom handle fan's any use to a man
and he's doing his bit for defence.

You need the U.S. to get out of this mess
once we're armed, no one will defeat us

SIR HIRAM MAXIM
But I have no machine against Haber's chlorine.

HUDSON MAXIM
Yeah, it might cool a few hot señoritas.

The only way out against gas-equipped Kraut
is to concoct a gas even worse
not be shocked into concocting
a fan that wouldn't get two farts to disperse.

53

He knew after Ypres that the cock of the heap
was no longer Sir Hiram Maxim
and whenever he thinks of that cloud with its stinks
a fit of coughing attacks him.

And then he seeks release in his *Pipe of Peace*
an invention it seems now more likely to last
for the paradox is that the great crowd that flocks
to inhale it are those who've been gassed.

In fact the demand has got out of hand
as Haber's invention gave Hiram's a boost.
Inhalers sell fast to those who've been gassed
who need more *Pipes of Peace* than produced.

SIR HIRAM MAXIM
This gas that I smoke whenever I choke
show gases are for good and for ill.
The many appealing for my gas that is healing
are those who breathed the Hun's gas that can kill.

Did the poison seep into the earth of Ypres
Will there ever again be flowers?

HUDSON MAXIM
The Hun's got gas devices, so my advice is
we'd better act quick and get ours!

If you poison their air then you'll be square
but make sure that you win the next round,
take the Hun by surprise and poison his skies
and show how his base deeds rebound.

Once the inventors let gas warfare enter
the destructive repertoire
you can't then put reins on inventive brains
whatever the protocols are.

You were very naïve if you could ever believe
that warfare would stop with your gun
for chemist/engineer a brand new era
of invention in war's just begun.

As he struggles for air he's becoming aware
that his own end may come any day.
His own death-rattle makes him weary of battle
but neither fan nor inhaler will keep death at bay.

SIR HIRAM MAXIM

No, while I still can I'll perfect this gas fan
and defend not go down the road
of gas escalation to annihilation
or the whole wretched world could explode.

My existence has meant I invent and invent
and I'm not going to stop now I'm fading.
I've got to create a gas-dissipator
in case the Hun ever thinks of invading.

HUDSON MAXIM

And that's what I'll say to the USA:
what if you're invaded? Prepare!
And be armed to repel these new forms of hell
these foul clouds of bright-coloured air.

And the vast population of the U.S. nation
will bring the whole world into line.

(HUDSON MAXIM *exits*.)

SIR HIRAM MAXIM

That Maximite he's claimed all night
as his gunpowder is mine.

My brother's gone away to the USA
to urge them again into arms.
But ever since Ypres even my sleep
has been haunted by gas alarms.

And what will THEY bring into the fray
if their inventors share my brother's view?
The worst nightmare of one starved of air
might be about to come true.

New inventors with weak consciences seek
to make better gas bombs than the Hun
War's taking off into chemical coughing
when I thought it had peaked with my gun.

(*The Gas Alarm 'music' begins slow and quiet.*)

The whole war long gas-klaxon, gas-gong
will become the new predominant sounds
and there'll be rapid increases in gas releases
now Fritz Haber has broken the bounds.

(*A fit of coughing. Inhales. Silence. Gas alarms louder. Puts
inhaler on floor and experiments with a gas fan. Stops. Silence.
Coughing. Picks up inhaler. Puts it down. Tries gas fan again.
Gas Alarm music.*)

Six BLIND GASSED SOLDIERS *enter, holding each other by the
shoulder. They are searching for the Pipe of Peace.*

SIR HIRAM MAXIM *coughs. The inhaler* (*the Pipe of Peace*)
*disintegrates. He coughs. Each cough has a ricochet of machine gun
fire. He puts his gloved hand over his mouth. He coughs and shoots
his hand with the cough. Out of the gloved hand stream red ribbons.*

*Gas Alarm Music louder. He flaps the gas fan frantically, then
drops it. He coughs. Each cough backs him upstage towards the
screen. He is retreating from what his invention has released into
the future. He backs through the back screen.*

*Enter Five flag-draped coffins on the revolve. The flags are two
Union Jacks, two German flags, one American.*

Gas Alarm Music.

Enter five SCIENTISTS *in gas masks and top hats, frock-coats etc.
They reprise their entry dance. They go one each to a coffin.
They attempt to make the coffin levitate. Nothing happens. Try
again. Hocus pocus. Nothing. They bend their heads. They
remove their top hats. Out of the top hats they begin 'magically'
to strew the white circle within the black rim revolve with
poppies. They try to levitate the coffins once more. Nothing.
They back away from the coffins until they touch centre.*

   *They turn towards the audience. They stare. They retreat
together through the black screen.*

*The Gas Alarm Music increases. From out of the five coffins
draped with flags the five* SCIENTISTS *(without gas masks) spring
as the Gas Alarm Music reaches a crescendo, and then at the next
moment they scatter out of the circle in all directions.*

*Gas Alarm Music louder and louder. Five silk clouds of different
colours, representing poisonous gases, appear in the sky. Off-
stage we hear voices singing beautifully the chemical names and
formulae of the gases. They sing:*

DI–CHLOR–O–DI–ETHYL SULPHIDE

(mustard gas/yellow silk, ending with:)

HYDROGEN CYANIDE – ZYKLON B

Enter six GAS-MASKED SOLDIERS, *with gas alarms hung on
rough tripods on three sticks lashed together. The alarms are
made from oil drums, shell cases, frying pans, bells. A rough
structure with a hanging gong inscribed 'gas alarm' flies into the
circle and is struck by the six* SOLDIERS. *As they play they
revolve and pass once behind the central gong still playing a
pandemonium of Gas Alarms.*

   *The Gas Alarm Music is slowly transformed into Chinese Music
and and slowly the* SOLDIERS *are transformed into* CHINESE

57

MUSICIANS *playing metal tubes, gongs, etc., shaped like the gas alarms only magically transformed into Chinese instruments. The central gong structure is transformed into a Chinese pagoda. The six* CHINESE MUSICIANS *are dressed in the black silk of nitrogen and the white silk of oxygen.*

From the Pagoda emerges the CHINESE MAGICIAN. *He summons the chlorine gas cloud out of the sky. It falls. He catches it and emerges from it dressed in a costume made from chlorine gas silk. He summons from the Pagoda* THREE CHINAMEN *in chlorine gas silk. This process is repeated with the five remaining silk gas clouds and each time the* CHINESE MAGICIAN *changes the colour of his costume and summons from the Pagoda* THREE CHINAMEN *until the entire company are on stage as* CHINAMEN *seated in positions which square the black circle. The Chinese Festival begins with music, dancing, juggling etc., ending with the presentation of 'Square Rounds' (circular hoops which transform into squares). Then the song begins.*

CHINAMEN

Silks bright and gay from ancient Cathay
and music redeeming the terror
but why we appear magically here
is to put the West right in its error.

We know the West thinks oh child-like Chinks
they invented gunpowder but employ
explosives in play like the firework display
but use something destructive for joy.

Sound the big gong, the West has been wrong
we all had the weapons you still use today.
Rocket, gas, gun, yes, every one
was pioneered in ancient Cathay.

CHINAMAN I

Festive creation and fiery devastation
both grew from the same bamboo.

58

It flung ammunition but for the musician
it was just a sweet flute that he blew.

CHINAMEN 2, 3 AND 4

From this bamboo all weapons grew
all those you in the West claim as yours.
Aeons and aeons before Europeans
we'd made use of them all in our wars.

CHINAMAN 5

From one tube of wood comes the bad and the good
The music that gladdens the heart,
the haunting sweet flute and something to shoot
a projectile that blows you apart.

CHINAMEN 6, 7 AND 8

From this bamboo all weapons grew
we had people blown up and gassed.
Every invention you were so proud to mention
is a 1000 years in the past.

(*The* CHINESE CHORUS *sing while the following is spoken
rhythmically.*)

CHINAMAN 9

Dried human dung was also flung
the first toxic smoke bomb in war.
It gets in the chinks of armour and stinks
and blisters the skin till it's raw.

CHINAMAN 10

Yes, we learned how to fling what we call *jen ching*
and with a bamboo bazooka hurled
what is plain shit to you (and human shit too)
the first toxic bomb in the world.

CHINAMAN I TO 21

Yes, we learned how to fling what we call *jen ching*

59

and with a bamboo bazooka hurled
what is plain shit to you (and human shit too)
the first toxic bomb in the world.

(*All throw red ribbons which 'explode' confetti over the
audience.*
   The CHINESE MAGICIAN *walks down with the black top hat.
Some poppy petals fall from it on to the white stage.*)

CHINAMAN I TO 21

(*Singing*)

To you it appears that all pioneers
of science were men who wore these
but all that you've seen, munition, machine,
had all been first made by Chinese.

The first rocket occurred when we took a bird
and harnessed fire to its claws.
These expendable doves set fire to foes' roofs
and helped us to win many wars.

As soon as a claw touched the roofing straw
it blazed and the blazes soon spread
the flames were fanned and got out of hand
and the poor bird was the first to fall dead.

The first missile to fly in the Chinese sky
was a flame attached to a dove
and if you want to end wars free the flame from its claws
and release it as Peace and as Love.

Now by slow stages through ages and ages
the rockets fly faster and higher
the problem is now to find a way how
to free the first dove from the fire.

CHINESE MAGICIAN

Now by slow stages through ages and ages

60

the rockets fly faster and higher
the problem is now to find a way how
to free the first dove from the fire.

(*The* CHINESE MAGICIAN *takes fire from the top hat and
transforms it into a bird.*

*They watch the bird fly into 1992. They begin to back, with
horror, upstage, trailing the red ribbons from their hands.
They back slowly into the back centre shutter. The* CHINESE
MAGICIAN *enters the Pagoda. The Pagoda explodes. The
company vanish in an instant. In place of the Pagoda is the Toilet
Cabin.*

Into the smoke, coughing, comes SWEEPER MAWES. *He is
sweeping up all the scattered poppies into red heaps. When he
has swept them all together, he goes to open the Toilet Cabin
door, recoils as if from a bad smell. He picks up the discarded
gas fan and flaps it furiously at the Toilet Cabin door. The*
SHELL-SHOCKED MAN *comes out of the Toilet Cabin with a dead
bird in his hand. He walks up the centre gangway of the theatre
and exits.*

Then SWEEPER MAWES, *using the gas fan as an improvised
shovel, sweeps the red heaps of the poppies together, shovels
them up and puts them down the toilet bowl.*)

SWEEPER MAWES
Toilet cabins! Whatever next?

*He looks round, enters the Toilet Cabin. After a moment we hear
a thunderous flush in which are the sounds, the drowned sounds,
of the whole play in recall.*

*Lights dim. Then go up again. The stage is empty as at the
beginning.*

THE END

The N and O Song

(Round in 3 parts)

Text:
Tony Harrison

Music:
Dominic Muldowney

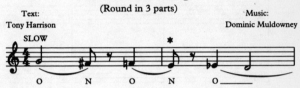

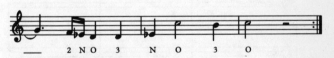

Text © 1992 by Tony Harrison
Music © 1992 by Faber Music Ltd.

The T N T Song

(Canon in 8 parts)

Text:
Tony Harrison

Music:
Dominic Muldowney

65

REPEAT AS OFTEN AS REQUIRED

66

67

Mourning Chorus

(Canon in 4 parts)

Text:
Tony Harrison

Music:
Dominic Muldowney

Text © 1992 by Tony Harrison
Music © 1992 by Faber Music Ltd.